Crowdfunding Scenarios Explained

CROWDFUNDING
SCENARIOS
Explained

If, How, and When to
Tax Money
from Crowdfunding

DELMAR C. GILLETTE

NEW YORK

LONDON • NASHVILLE • MELBOURNE • VANCOUVER

Crowdfunding Scenarios Explained

If, How, and When to Tax Money from Crowdfunding

© 2018 Delmar C. Gillette

Published in New York, New York, by Morgan James Publishing. Morgan James is a trademark of Morgan James, LLC. www. MorganJamesPublishing.com

The Morgan James Speakers Group can bring authors to your live event. For more information or to book an event visit The Morgan James Speakers Group at www.TheMorganJamesSpeakersGroup.com.

ISBN 9781683508595 paperback
ISBN 9781683508601 eBook
Library of Congress Control Number: 2017917954

Cover Design by:
Rachel Lopez
www.r2cdesign.com

Interior Design by:
Chris Treccani
www.3dogcreative.net

In an effort to support local communities, raise awareness and funds, Morgan James Publishing donates a percentage of all book sales for the life of each book to Habitat for Humanity Peninsula and Greater Williamsburg.

Get involved today! Visit www.MorganJamesBuilds.com

TABLE OF CONTENTS

Foreword   vii
Introduction   ix

A Historical View   1
Traditional Funding   5
A Crowdfunding Primer   9
To Crowdfund or Not: Pros and Cons   18
Types of Crowdfunding   23
Crowdfunding and Taxes   25
Crowdfunding Participants   29
The Trouble Between Form 1099-MISC
        and Form 1099-K   33
Crowdfunding and Taxes: Case Studies   41
Crowdfrauding   60
Avoiding Crowdfunding Scams   63
Endnotes   74

FOREWORD

It can't be true! That large contribution I made to a GOFundMe account is NOT deductible on my tax return!

This book written by Delmar C. Gillette explains crowdfunding regulations, rules, advantages/hazards, and choices, etc.

I became acquainted with Mr. Gillette (Delmar) over 25 years ago when I joined the National Association of Tax Professionals (NATP) back in 1989. At that time, Delmar was an instructor for NATP. We also both served at the chapter level of the Virginia Chapter/NATP. Delmar was very active in the Chapter (President/Vice President). I was Executive Director of the Virginia Chapter at that time and called on Delmar many, many times to be an instructor at the chapter level. Delmar willingly taught year after year, on various subjects, for our yearly conferences and meetings. His knowledge of the tax laws, and applications to everyday life, proved invaluable. Chapter members always asked for his return as an instructor.

In this book, Delmar writes in detail about Crowdfunding from determining if the gift is taxable to the recipient, to the consequences of the Form 1099-K, to understanding the pros and cons of crowdfunding. He writes, in great detail, about the growth and complexity of crowdfunding in terms that a "regular individual" can understand.

I was particularly interested in the section of the article where Delmar described how a Crowdfunding project turned from a dream to a nightmare. The five situations presented were unbelievable.

I was so honored that Delmar asked me to write the foreword for this book. I jumped at the chance to do this—and thank Delmar for giving me this opportunity.

Teresa C. Steiniger, Accountant, EA

INTRODUCTION

Crowdfunding. For the readers who are part of the "baby boomer" generation this term may evoke the question, "What is crowdfunding?" For the millennials, it may be as familiar as Twitter, Snapchat, and Instagram, and bring to mind names like Kickstarter, IndieGoGo, and GoFundMe.

Crowdfunding is, by definition, "the practice of funding a project or venture by raising many small amounts of money from a large number of people, typically via the Internet."[1] A common misconception is that crowdfunding is a modern creation. Indeed, the first recent recorded instance of crowdfunding occurred in 1997, when a British rock band (*Marillion*) funded their reunion tour through online donations from fans. Inspired by this innovative method of financing, ArtistShare became the first dedicated crowdfunding platform in 2000. Shortly thereafter, more crowdfunding platforms began to emerge, and the crowdfunding industry has grown consistently each year.[2]

There are two terms, crowdfunding and crowdsourcing, that appear to be often confused. They are not the same thing. *Crowdsourcing* is the online gathering of a group of people to share knowledge and wisdom to build a better product. It started with "open source" computer software where companies allowed freelance programmers to "clean up, fix, and/or otherwise improve the code. In another example, the online encyclopedia of sorts, Wikipedia, is crowdsourcing where anyone is free to edit and allow the crowd's wisdom to fill the pages. From this concept is was only a matter of time before the community moved into the financial arena as crowdfunding.[3]

A HISTORICAL VIEW

However, the concept of "crowdfunding" has a much longer history. An example is found in the Bible (NIV) Acts 3:2, "Now a man who was lame from birth was being carried to the temple gate called Beautiful, where he was put every day to beg from those going into the temple courts." This reference meets the classical definition of "crowdfunding", funding a project by raising many small amounts of money from a large number of people. There are other such examples.

In 1713, Alexander Pope set out to translate 15,693 lines of ancient Greek poetry into English. It took five long years to get the six volumes right, but the result was worth the wait: a translation of Homer's *Iliad* that endures to this day. How did Pope go about getting this project off the ground?

Pope crafted his pitch: "This Work shall be printed in six Volumes in Quarto, on the finest Paper, and on a letter new Cast on purpose; with Ornaments and initial Letters engraven on Copper." In exchange for a shout-out in the acknowledgements, an early edition of the book, and the delight of helping to bring a new creative work into the world, 750 subscribers pledged two gold guineas to support Pope's effort before he put pen to paper. They were listed in an early edition of the book.[4]

In 1783, Mozart took a similar path. He wanted to perform three recently composed piano concertos in a Viennese concert hall, and he published an invitation to prospective backers offering manuscripts to those who pledged:

"These three concertos, which can be performed with full orchestra including wind instruments, or only a Quattro, that is with 2 violins, 1 viola and violoncello, will be available at the beginning of April to those who have subscribed for them (beautifully copied, and supervised by the composer himself)."[5]

Alas, not all projects reach their funding goals, and Mozart fell short. A year later he tried again, and 176 backers pledged enough to bring his concertos to life. He thanked them in the concertos' manuscript by publishing their names.[6]

In 1885, arguably the most ambitious project of all to find funding this way began. France was at work on a statue of the Roman goddess of freedom to give to the United States to celebrate its centennial. But the Statue of Liberty had no pedestal on which to stand in New York Harbor. Joseph Pulitzer, publisher of *The New York World*, launched a project for the construction of one.

Pulitzer published the project in his newspaper and offered rewards to supporters. For $1 a backer would get a six-inch statuette of Lady Liberty. More than 120,000 people from around the world pledged $102,006 to the project.[7]

An interesting scholarly report, "A Brief History of Crowdfunding" by David M Freedman and Matthew R Nutting, can be found easily on the internet.[8] Freedman has served on the editorial staff of The Value Examiner since 2005, and is a contributing writer for the Accredited Investor Markets. Nutting practices corporate law, is a director of the National Crowdfunding Association and cofounder of CrowdPassage.

So, the theme of "crowdfunding" has been around for hundreds, if not thousands, of years, but has not been until recently a primary method of acquiring capital for various projects. Where else does money come from?

TRADITIONAL FUNDING

Some of the more traditional methods of funding a project have included Angels, VC (venture capital), commercial banks, and bootstrapping. In an article by Christa Avampatao, these methods are described.[9]

- Briefly, an <u>Angel</u> investor helps a good idea get off the ground by providing the necessary cash for launch in exchange for a piece of ownership, or equity, in the company.
- <u>Venture capital</u> (VC), unlike angel investments, is funding provided through a professionally managed fund and is typically for a larger amount of money than an angel investment. VC funding usually comes into play after a business has gotten off the ground.

- <u>Commercial Loans</u> – Loans obtained from commercial banks or other financial institutions.
- <u>Bootstrap</u> defines the use of personal funds as well as those from friends and family. Interestingly both Dell and Facebook received their initial funding through bootstrapping.[10]

Angels, venture capital, commercial loans and bootstrapping take time to develop as the entrepreneurs need budgets, forecasts, and studies of feasibility of the concept to attract the capital they need. We can see the concept of Angel and venture capital in a broadcast program called "Shark Tank." A rotating cast of six "angels" listen to the pitch of aspiring entrepreneurs and make offers (or not) based on their individual business experiences and deep pockets. In exchange for a percentage of the business they make an offer of cash. From time to time two or more "sharks" may combine to make an offer.[11] As with most traditional funding, there is but one or two sources of capital – the large firms represented by the sharks.

So why crowdfunding? Thanks to the internet, and social media in particular, it is possible today to reach large audiences with your proposed product or idea and receive funding from huge numbers of individuals. While there are still hurdles to conquer (how to set up a crowdfunding platform, how to receive the funds, will my product attract attention, and will it sell?) there can be significant rewards of crowdfunding.

Our Topics

In this booklet we are going to examine:

1. The concepts of crowdfunding,
2. the various facets of organizations of crowdfunding,
3. several details about how crowdfunding works,
4. the emergence of a huge oversight by the IRS with Form 1099-MISC and 1099-K,
5. examples of potential crowdfunding tax issues,
6. how to identify possible scams and frauds, and
7. how you as the tax professional can bring comfort to crowdfunding individuals.

A CROWDFUNDING PRIMER

Let's take a look at how the process of modern crowdfunding works in general. To keep things simple, we'll focus on the two most popular types of crowdfunding, Donation Crowdfunding and Rewards-based Crowdfunding.

A Crowdfunding Creator

1. **You have an idea for a project that may benefit from crowdfunding:**
   a. If your project is to raise money for a cause, with no tangible rewards to the backer, you'll use Donation Crowdfunding. Backers will give money to support the need you've identified.
   b. If your project involves the creation of a physical good (a cooking utensil, phone accessory, board game) or digital good (music album, digital film, or software),

you may choose to use Rewards-based Crowdfunding.

2. **You create a listing for your project on one (or more) of the dozens of different crowdfunding sites, choosing one that matches your method of crowdfunding. You'll include a narrative about your project, perhaps video and photo content, and the site will facilitate the gathering of funds from backers.**

   a. For Donation Crowdfunding, that's about all your listing needs.

   b. For Rewards-based Crowdfunding, you'll create levels of support that each have unique rewards for the backer, and are each limited to a certain number of backers. These often include (and may be combined at various levels):

      i. A discount on the product's eventual market price, often 25-40%. There may be multiple levels of discount, with the first backers getting the best deal.

ii. Early delivery of the product, before it's made available to the public, often by 3-6 months or more. Again, this may be in stages, so first backers get the product in the first round of production/delivery.

iii. Collateral material, or "swag", related to the product – a sticker, keychain, apparel, or other special accessory.

iv. Special mention as a supporter in the product's packaging, or in the credits for a digital good.

v. Experiential rewards for huge amounts (often $10,000 or more) of support:

1. A culinary product might reward you with dinner for 4, prepared by the chef behind the product.

2. An entertainment product, such as a movie, might cast you in a role as an extra in the film.

3. **You publicize your crowdfunding project** in as many ways as possible, generally focusing on social media channels (Twitter, Facebook, etc.) so that others will help spread the word about your project. You'll also likely provide updates along the way, so your backers can see the progress of your project.

4. **You use the funds you receive (minus fees from the crowdfunding platform) to achieve your project's purpose.**

   a. For Donation Crowdfunding, this means sending the money to assist with the need you've identified, or purchasing the goods or services that will serve that need.

   b. For Rewards-based Crowdfunding, this means creating your product (paying for research, development, prototyping, testing, manufacturing, quality testing, and shipping to backers).

5. **You decide on the next step:**

a. For Donation Crowdfunding, there often isn't a next step, as you've met the need you originally intended to.

b. For Rewards-based Crowdfunding, you may move to full-scale production and distribution of your product, or have your product bought out by a larger, more established company, or decide to make improvements and launch another Crowdfunding project.

A Crowdfunding Backer

1. **You become aware of the crowdfunding project,** perhaps through social media (a tweet, a Facebook post, etc.), a news article, or by browsing the crowdfunding site itself.

2. **You read about the proposed project/ product/goal, and decide to participate.**

3. **You choose your level of support, and make your payment:**

   a. For Donation Crowdfunding (for medical expense assistance, disaster relief, etc.) you make a donation in the amount that suits you;

   a.   For Rewards-based Crowdfunding, often used for new physical goods, you choose from a series of increasing amounts, each offering special rewards or discounts.

4. **You wait.**
   a.   For Donation Crowdfunding, you wait to see if the goal is met, and hopefully get updates on what the money was used for after the fact. Your process ends here.
   b.   For Rewards-based Crowdfunding, you wait and watch for updates on the development and production of the product you're supporting. In some cases, you may receive early rewards before the product is launched (such as a T-shirt, or sticker, or other method of promoting and marketing the product).
5. **(Ideally,) the product is delivered.**

Funding Options

Rather than just throwing your money into an unknown crowdfunding idea; what is happening with your money? If the project is not supported by the general public, what happens to your money?

There are two general methods regarding your purchase or contribution. They are:

- **Flexible Funding: Keep Your Money No Matter What**

    Choose flexible funding if any amount of money will help you reach your campaign objective and you'll still be able to fulfill your perks. Flexible funding is suitable for almost all the campaigns on Indiegogo. With flexible funding, you keep all funds, even if you do not meet your goal!

- **Fixed Funding: Keep Your Money Only If You Meet Your Goal**

    If flexible funding doesn't seem right for you and you have a strict go/no-go threshold, you can run a fixed funding campaign instead. With a fixed funding campaign, you only keep the funds you raise **if** you meet your funding goal. If your campaign does not meet its goal by its deadline, all contributions will be refunded back to the contributors by the crowdfunding platform, typically within 5-7 business days.[12] (This method is also called "all or none" funding.)

A new study, from Toronto's York University and Université Lille Nord de France in Lille, France, compares the results of those two different types of crowdfunding campaigns. The report's researchers looked at 22,875 crowdfunding campaigns, each of which was trying to raise between $5,000 and $200,000. They pulled the information from Indiegogo, since that site is both large and well established, and lets entrepreneurs choose either a keep-it-all or an all-or-nothing campaign. Those who used the keep-it-all model were trying, on average, to raise $19,677. Those who went all-or-nothing, on average, were trying to raise more: $31,355.

Yet the all-or-nothing folks were more likely to hit their fundraising goals: 34 percent of their campaigns were successfully completed, compared to 17 percent of the keep-it-all campaigns. All-or-nothing campaigns attracted an average of 188 backers, while on average the keep-it-all variety attracted 73.[13]

TO CROWDFUND OR NOT: PROS AND CONS

Crowdfunding is beneficial because it:[14]

- **Saves Time and Money:** Instead of doing endless rounds of banks and the offices of private investors, you can organize your crowdfunding strategy very quickly.

- **Gives You Access to Capital:** It takes significantly lesser time than raising capital via traditional means. Usually, a fundraising campaign has a maximum cap of 90 days. This eliminates the need for constant pitching, prospecting, negotiating etc., which is the case when you obtain funds from banks and other financial institutions. In addition, you do not necessarily have to give up equity in your company either. Instead, you could offer reward-based incentives to your investors. You do not need to pay any fees upfront either.

- **Helps You Establish a Customer Base:** Finding customers initially can be tough for a new business. However, if you've raised funds through crowdfunding, you effectively have a large group of people backing your offering. As a result, many of your investors do not just become your customers, but they also become an extension of your sales force as they promote your business through their own social media connections. This is useful for bringing in additional customers. Crowdfunding also helps you engage with your customers, giving you a direct line of contact with them through the platform. It's possible to get feedback early-on in the process through prospective backers.

- **Helps You Organize Your Marketing Strategy:** When you seek crowdfunding for your business idea, you are effectively promoting your idea to others. This is in addition to seeking funding. Once you generate the funds required, you will have a clearer idea about how to make your marketing strategy more effective. In short, the clarity of the message that got you the funding will also help you attract your customers.

- **Gives You Control Over How to Reward Your Investors:** Once you receive the funding required, you get to determine how to reward your investors. As long as you're reasonable, you have complete control over how much equity or interest you can offer your investors.

Some feel crowdfunding is not viable because it:

- **Does Not Deliver for Business-to-Business Offerings:** People generally back something because they identify with it or perceive some benefits from it. As a result, they will back offerings aimed at consumers, instead of at business entities.

- **Does Not Work for Complex Projects:** Crowdfunding works if the business idea is simple enough for the layperson to understand. Complex or technical projects might come a cropper if they seek crowdfunding. Even projects with lengthy research-and-development cycles could draw people away from investing in your idea.

- **Might Not Fund Large Capital Requirements:** Barring exceptions, crowdfunding typically works for projects that require under $100,000 of capital. If your idea requires larger funding, you might need to consider looking at other traditional sources for raising capital, e.g banks, etc.

- **Often Follows an All-or-Nothing Approach:** Some crowdfunding platforms only release the funds from your campaign once your campaign achieves 100 percent or more of its funding goal. As such, you could be stuck in limbo if your campaign fails to achieve its target funding.
- **Makes Your Project Inflexible:** Once you receive the funding you need, you cannot make drastic changes to your offering. Similarly, any delays in timelines could damage your reputation and hurt your brand.
- **Exposes Your Idea to Copycats:** You risk the chance of having your product or idea ripped off, as the product is being advertised before actually hitting the market. Trademarks and patents do provide some defensibility, but they are hard to enforce internationally.[15]

TYPES OF CROWDFUNDING

Depending upon who you ask, there are three to six (or more) styles of crowdfunding. Let's quickly look at these:

1. <u>Donation Crowdfunding</u> – people invest because they believe in the cause (medical expenses, house fires, extraordinary expenses, etc.)[16]

2. <u>Debt crowdfunding</u> – investors receive the principal along with interest. This is similar to a loan offered by banks, but different in that investors have the benefit of contributing toward the success of an idea they believe in.[17]

3. <u>Equity crowdfunding</u> – people invest in the project in exchange for equity. In return for the money they invest, they receive a share in the business, project or venture. If the project becomes successful,

the value of their share increases. If the project fails to achieve the desired results, the investors could even end up losing the amount invested.[18]

4. <u>Reward-based crowdfunding</u>: You receive a reward in exchange for your support of a project. This type of crowdfunding has been used for purposes such as motion picture production and promotion, the production and release of musical albums and CDs, software development, the development of inventions, scientific research, and civic projects.

5. <u>Royalty crowdfunding</u>: Royalty crowdfunding offers backers a percentage of revenue from the project or venture the backer supports, once it is generating capital. A good example of this approach is a mobile app website where backers can support an app before it's fully developed or launched, and then share in the revenue once the app starts selling to the public.[19]

CROWDFUNDING AND TAXES

At this point, as a tax preparer or tax professional you may be asking, 'Why do I care about Crowdfunding?"

First, in the Massolution Crowdfunding Industry 2015 Report, they write, "Total Global Crowdfunding Industry estimated fundraising volume was $34 Billion" (with North America being nearly 50% of that total.)[20]

Second, the Internal Revenue Service (IRS) has released <u>zero</u> rules and <u>zero</u> regulations regarding how to deal with the myriad of tax issues in crowdfunding. It is difficult to comprehend why a cash industry as large as $34 billion is being ignored by the IRS.

Third, as a tax practitioner or tax professional it seems reasonable that you want to be proficient in dealing with the topic and tax issues of crowdfunding.[21, 22]

Fourth, the <u>annual</u> rate of growth of crowdfunding from 2012 to 2015 was over 73%! (From $2.7B to $34.4B)[23]

Fifth, with the volume of annual growth, it is reasonable to assume that crowdfunding is not going away in the near future and that the tax issues will grow with it.

Sixth, with such attractive ability to raise money from crowdfunding, might fraudsters or scammers be interested in taking advantage of people?

The answer is an obvious "yes" and we will touch on how to recognize scams in the same way we try to educate our clients about scammers and the IRS. Even the financial media is beginning to recognize that not only could entrepreneurs use a bit of guidance with crowdfunding due to the potential tax traps for unwary individuals, but tax professionals like yourself could also use additional education. Experts warn that the issue of whether a recipient's windfall is considered a gift or income could be a gray area.[24]

In a related concern, a different style business track is developing – The On-Demand Economy.

Think Uber. Startups like Uber achieved massive success not by inventing new products or categories, but by disrupting the way industries operate, and making our lives more convenient in the process. Companies like Uber succeed by putting information at our fingertips and giving us what we want: instant gratification.[25] There are many other on-demand companies, Buddytruk, StyleBee, Dispatch, Airbnb, TaskRabbit, and Etsy to name only a few. These companies are not crowdfunding activities, rather they perform a skill and provide prompt service. The IRS already recognizes this on-demand economy and has created a specific location on its website for this: Sharing Economy Tax Center (another name for on-demand).[26] The reason the IRS took this step, in my opinion, is that it was simpler to understand than crowdfunding. They see the sharing economy clearly as a 1099-MISC business, but as we'll learn later, the 1099-MISC and the 1099-K forms and instructions are in conflict with each other. Even now, articles are being written about the concept of "Will There Be an Uber for the Accounting Profession?"

But, alas, there is not yet a crowdfunding page on the IRS website. To my specific point – a tax practitioner has set up a website to cater to these On-Demand businesses. $hared Economy CPA[27] has already received great press from CPATrends, United States Senate, Time, AccountingToday, Fortune and others. Interestingly enough, $hared Economy CPA is actually part of the on-demand or shared economy process. Their blog is full of helpful information for the participants of the on-demand or shared economy. Imagine if you could set up a website to funnel interest in helping crowdfunders prepare their tax returns, offer advice on how best to choose a platform and the myriad of other things we are wanting to bring to your knowledge.

CROWDFUNDING PARTICIPANTS

Now that you understand reasons why being knowledgeable about crowdfunding is important, there are some other terms or vocabulary we need to discuss before we move to the taxation of crowdfunding. Before discussing the tax issues associated with a crowdfunding campaign, the taxpayers involved with the campaign need to be identified:

- Creator. The creator of a crowdfunding campaign is the individual or organization that sets up the project and seeks donations from the crowd. In general crowdfunding terms, the creator could be both the person who sets up the project and the one who directly benefits from the donations. For purposes of the rest of this discussion, the term creator is used only to describe a person who sets up the project for someone or something else. If such person also benefits from the donations, that person is described as the recipient.

- <u>Donor or investor</u>. The terms donor and investor are tax terms. In crowdfunding, donors and investors are referred to as backers. The backer is the person who donates, invests, or contributes funds to the cause, project, or venture. For purposes of the rest of this discussion, the tax term donor is used to describe the one providing funds for a project, unless the donor receives some type of ownership interest in the project, in which case the term investor is used.

- <u>Recipient</u>. The recipient is the one who benefits from the project or campaign. The recipient may also be referred to as the donee or beneficiary, which are tax terms. In crowdfunding, the donee, beneficiary, or recipient is referred to either as the project, creator (when the creator is the one who receives the funds), or campaign. For purposes of the rest of this discussion, the term recipient is used to describe the person or business or organization that receives the funds that are raised.

• <u>Platform</u>. The platform is the moderating organization that brings the parties together to launch the idea. For online crowdfunding, the platform is the website that allows the creator to set up a campaign to find donors or investors who are willing to provide funds for a recipient.[28] (Popular examples include Kickstarter, Indiegogo, RocketHub, GoFundMe, and there are hundreds more.)

And of course, there are fees, which can range from zero up to 20%. That's just on the money collected. Depending upon whether you meet your goal or not, your fees can be higher. Then there is a credit card processing fee ranging from 1% to 4% plus a per-charge fee. Some sites have a set-up fee. Sites claiming to be "100% Free" will charge your donors up to 15% and you'll still need to pay 3% for processing.[29] In a blog article "How Much Does it Cost to Run a Crowdfunding Campaign?"[30] Joe Recomendes takes a crowdfunder through the range of fees – product design, prototype manufacturing, photography and video, expos, trade shows, and pounding the pavement, advertising, press release distribution, marketing consultant, paying the platform, rewards, manufacturing, and fulfillment.

Before going forward, there is a current situation with how payments are made to crowdfunding platforms and how that information is reported to the creator. We call it "The Trouble between Form 1099-MISC and Form 1099-K."

THE TROUBLE BETWEEN FORM 1099-MISC AND FORM 1099-K

For decades, many tax practitioners and taxpayers knew about the purpose of Form 1099-MISC.[31] It is a reporting document for the following payments to taxpayers:

- at least $10 in royalties or broker payments in lieu of dividends or tax-exempt interest;
- at least $600 in:
  - rents;
  - services performed by someone who is not your employee;
  - prizes and awards;
  - other income payments;
  - medical and health care payments;
  - crop insurance proceeds;
  - cash payments for fish (or other aquatic life) you purchase from

> anyone engaged in the trade or business of catching fish;
> - generally, the cash paid from a notional principal contract to an individual, partnership, or estate;
> - payments to an attorney; or
> - any fishing boat proceeds.

In addition, use this form to report that you made direct sales of at least $5,000 of consumer products to a buyer for resale anywhere other than a permanent retail establishment.

In 2008, the Housing and Economic Recovery Act (HERA 2008), the bill to kick start the declining housing market, was passed. Tucked in the middle of the housing bill was a provision that had absolutely nothing to do with housing. It was a new requirement that banks and credit card merchants report payments to the IRS on a new form and the instructions for Form 1099-MISC were changed.[32]

The instructions indicate that the form 1099-MISC is not to be issued if payments are made "with a credit card or payment card and certain other types of payments, including third party network transactions."

In simple terms, taxpayers who have a credit card merchant account, Paypal account or similar account and otherwise meet the criteria will receive Form 1099-K from their service providers. That would include professionals like lawyers and architects who accept online or credit card payments for services, freelancers compensated via PayPal, Etsy sellers, affiliates, eBay merchants and other small businesses who accept credit cards, debit card or PayPal as payment.

> *Payments made with a credit card or payment card and certain other types of payments, including third party network transactions, must be reported on Form 1099-K by the payment settlement entity under section 6050W and are not subject to reporting on Form 1099-MISC. (emphasis added)33*

Remember, the original purpose of the new Form 1099-K was to "improve voluntary tax compliance by business taxpayers and help the IRS determine if their tax returns were complete and correct."

If you made $20,000 or more in the taxable year in 200 or more transactions from one payment processor, then you get the 1099-K. If you don't fit <u>both</u> of those criteria, you don't get Form 1099-K. If you made $20,000 but in only 199 transactions the new form won't come your way. But in either case, if payments to the taxpayer were by credit card or similar payment, no 1099-MISC is required.

If you made $50,000 in 500 transactions and you only sell on Amazon, then Amazon will send you a 1099-K. If you made $20,000 in 200 transactions but that was spread out over Square, Amazon, and PayPal, then you should not receive Form 1099-K. What if the aforementioned $20,000 is actually $50,000 but all of the merchants received less than $20,000 in payments for any one merchant? According to the rules there is no requirement for Form 1099-K. And in any of these cases, if payments to the taxpayer were by credit card or similar payment, no 1099-MISC is required.

Form 1099-K includes your gross sales for the year, but doesn't take into account things like sales tax or shipping fees collected, fees from your payment processor, and refunds or returns. That's why it's important to keep track of your income and expenses on your own, too.

These 3rd party payment processors also send this information to the IRS, too. So don't ignore this form![34]

In response to questions for better clarity, the IRS issued this statement:[35]

> "A third party settlement organization is required to report any information concerning third party network transactions of any participating payee only if, for the calendar year:
>
> The gross amount of total reportable payment transactions exceeds $20,000, and the total number of such transactions exceeds 200.

If a business makes payments via a third party settlement organization as well as cash or check to the same independent contractor, the TPSO (third party settlement organization) will be required to report the amount of reportable transactions that exceed the de minimis thresholds on Form 1099-K. The amounts paid by cash or check would be reported by the business on Form 1099-MISC, if the amounts are $600 or more in a calendar year.

The regulations state that reportable payments made under Section 6050W are not reportable under Section 6041. If reportable payments under Section 6050W do not meet the de minimis thresholds in a calendar year, no reporting is required. (Section 6050W is the section of the Tax Code which spells out the reporting provisions for "payments made in settlement of payment card and third party network transactions.")

We are aware of a potential for 1099-MISC and 1099-K double reporting, and are constantly monitoring our case selection criteria to address this. We do expect to provide more guidance, but we also do not expect this issue to lead to an increase in examinations."

So, taking all of these together, it's clear that payments reported on a form 1099-K are not also reportable on form 1099-MISC – which makes sense. However, if the payments don't meet the thresholds for reporting on the form 1099-K and would be otherwise reportable, no reporting is required – which doesn't make as much sense. There is a case if less than $20,000 in payments or less than 200 transactions that no 1099-K is required. However, if the payments would have been reportable except for the de minimums requirements, no 1099-MISC is required.

Thus if a taxpayer has over $600 of payments for goods or services, but all were paid by a credit card, there is no requirement for Form 1099-MISC to be filed. If a taxpayer has less than $20,000 in payments, but only 199 transactions, there is no requirement for the PSEs to issue a 1099-K.

It turns out, that's right. But, doesn't that create a giant reporting hole? The IRS response: "*it was not an "inaccurate characterization.*"[36]

But what about that hole? That giant reporting hole? If the idea is to move folks into compliance, anyone that falls in that reporting hole has an incentive not to comply – and clearly, taxpayers are making a purposeful effort to fall into that hole to escape reporting.

Let's look at the match. Your payments of cash and checks is less than $601. Your credit card payments are less than $20,000 regardless of the number of transactions. So you have $20,000 – $601= $19,399. Can someone please tell me how this helps "improve voluntary tax compliance by business taxpayers and help the IRS determine if their tax returns were complete and correct?"

CROWDFUNDING AND TAXES: CASE STUDIES

Now that the basics are behind us, the most difficult tax question to answer when it comes to crowdfunding is whether or not the recipient is subject to tax on the receipt of funds that are raised. The simple answer is it all depends on the facts and circumstances. Substance over form determines the tax ramification of the transaction. To illustrate the problem, the following example is based on a real life crowdfunding campaign.[37]

Example #1:

Wanda owns a small corner café. She works hard to keep her business successful, and she has a small group of loyal customers who frequent her establishment. A tragic incident occurs in the neighborhood that provokes rioting and local businesses are burned and looted. The windows in Wanda's café are broken and vandals destroy tables, chairs, and kitchen equipment while looters steal her cash register, safe, and food inventory. A national talk show radio host provides publicity for Wanda's plight by describing her as a hard working small business owner who is the victim of senseless violence. Her business is at risk of failure due to the loss of business while she attempts to rebuild. The talk show host tells his listeners about a crowdfunding campaign set up to help Wanda. $100,000 is raised through the crowdfunding campaign with the proceeds going to Wanda.

- What are Wanda's tax ramifications on the receipt of the funds?
- Are they taxable as business income, taxable as other income, or are they considered tax-free gifts?

Under IRC section 61, gross income includes all income from whatever source derived, unless there is a specific Internal Revenue Code section that describes an exception, and the transaction meets the rules described in that code section and *applicable regulations. There is no specific code section that defines the tax treatment of funds received through a crowdfunding campaign. It is the substance of the crowdfunding transaction that determines the tax ramifications.*

The Internal Revenue Code lists the following exclusions from gross income: IRC §101-109, §111-112, §115, §117-119, §121-123, §125-127, §129-133, and §134-139A-F.

All of the above exclusions from gross income require specific details to apply before the exclusion is allowed. An exclusion from gross income applicable to crowdfunding campaigns could be the exclusion for gifts under IRC §102. Gross income does not include the value of property (including cash) acquired by gift, bequest, devise, or inheritance. The exclusion does not apply to income received from the gifted property. The exclusion also does not apply to gifts from an employer to an employee.[38]

The code and regulations do not define the term "gift," however, they do provide some examples. An amount of principal paid under a marriage settlement is a tax free gift, except for any amount that meets the definition of alimony under IRC § 71. The term gift also does not include prizes and awards, which are taxable under IRC § 74, except for certain employee achievement awards which are tax free under IRC § 74(c). A gift from an employer to an employee is taxable under IRC § 102(c), unless it meets the definition of a *de minimis* benefit under IRC § 132(e), such as a holiday gift that is not in cash and has a low fair market value.[39]

It is important not to confuse the exclusion of gifts under IRC § 102 with the deductibility of gifts to charity under IRC §170. Whether or not the donor of a gift can deduct it as a charitable contribution under IRC §170 has nothing to do with whether or not the recipient of the gift can exclude it from gross income under IRC §102. The two code sections are not tied together. A child, for example, is not a tax-exempt charity. Yet there is no question that cash gifts from a parent to a child are tax free to the child.[40]

With little guidance from the code and regulations, it is necessary to look to the courts for the definition of a tax free gift under IRC §102.

In *Berst, T.C. Memo. 1997- 137 (March 17, 1997)*, the Tax Court said property is considered a gift if given in a spirit of detached and disinterested generosity.[41]

In Caracci, *118 T.C. No. 25 (May 22, 2002)*, the Tax Court said when property is transferred for less than adequate and full consideration in money or money's worth, the amount by which the value of the property exceeds the value of the consideration is deemed a gift.

In Hamlett, *T.C. Memo. 2004-78 (March 22, 2004)*, the Tax Court said a gift is a transfer of property that proceeds from a detached and disinterested generosity, out of affection, respect, admiration, charity, or like impulses. The transferor's intent in making the transfer is the most critical consideration in determining whether the property transferred was a gift.

In Hatch, *T.C. Memo. 2012-50 (February 23, 2012)*, while acknowledging that transfers by or for an employer to an employee are not excludible from income under IRC §102(c), the Tax Court noted that in exceptional circumstances, a transfer between an employer and an employee may be considered a gift. The legislative history of section 102 indicates that a gift may be made by an employer to an employee if it is exclusively for personal reasons, if it is entirely unrelated to the employment relationship, and if it reflects no anticipation of business benefit.

With this example let's consider some interesting other comments about crowdfunding. Since the IRS has not released any guidance about the taxation of crowdfunding, we as tax practitioners and professionals need to have a deeper and clearer understanding of what is really going on.

To be totally fair, the IRS has issued Information Letter 2016-0036.[42] Unfortunately, the contents of this letter are about as useful as a compass without a magnetic needle. Consider the following. What is not terribly clear to many is what the tax treatment of a crowdsourcing program should be, especially given the wide variety instructions and conditions involved in such programs. The letter does not go into details. It states that the letter is for general information only and specifically if the taxpayer wants a specific ruling, go through the private letter ruling process. The letter did state that crowdfunding revenues are generally includible in income if not:

1. loans that need to be repaid,
2. capital contributed to an entity in exchange for an equity interest in the entity, or
3. gifts made out of detached generosity and without any "quid pro quo."

The letter concludes "the income tax consequences to a taxpayer of a crowdfunding effort depend upon all the facts and circumstances surrounding that effort." Where have we heard that expression before?

Here is the list of advice and concerns:

1. Crowdfunding proceeds are taxable income. (maybe)

Generally crowdfunding proceeds must be reported as income in the year you receive them, or they are constructively available to you.

Some people argue crowdfunding proceeds are gifts. However, if you don't know the people contributing and they receive something of value in return, that's going to be a difficult argument to make.

Many crowdfunding deals offer bigger items in return for larger "donations," which makes the gift argument even less tenable.

2. **You may owe state sales tax and income tax.**

Consider the expected income taxes for federal and state. But are you aware of the possibility of the following additional taxes: state business license, business license for the city and/or county, reseller certificate or exemption permit, city and/or county business taxes (fees), and use tax? You need to be aware of Internet sales tax rules. While Congress keeps kicking this "can" down the road, brick and mortar storefronts continue to feel that internet sales reduce their sales (lower costs for internet only sellers) and the added discount of no sales taxes added to the price. While many large sellers ($1 million or more) have started collecting the internet sales tax, not all states have adopted this rule. So even if your crowdfunding taxpayer has gross sales of less than $1 million you might want to check this site to see what your taxpayer's home state is doing: "Internet Sales Tax: A 50-State Guide to State Laws."[43]

3. **You can deduct expenses from income.**

4. **You may be able to deduct start-up expenses in the year you paid them.**

Some expenses for investigating the creation of a business or the actual start-up costs for a new business are not ordinarily deductible in the year you paid them.

While start-up expenses are generally considered capital expenditures and therefore amortized over the course of 180 months, the IRS does allow you to deduct up to $5,000 in the year the business begins.

That $5,000 is reduced dollar-for-dollar by your cumulative start-up expenses in excess of $50,000.

5. **Research and development costs merit special tax treatment.**

Research and experimental costs are generally your expenses to develop or improve a product. You can choose to amortize research and development costs over 10 years, or deduct them in the year you have the expense.

6. **Beware of raising crowdfunding proceeds late in the year.**

The problem: you can't report the income in the next year, nor can you deduct next year's expenses this year.

The best advice is to avoid such a scenario. Make sure you plan crowdfunding projects so you receive proceeds early enough in the year that you can hopefully match your expenses to your income.[44]

Note: discussion of the following examples, as well as additional scenarios and information, can be found on this booklets companion website: *www.crowdfundingtaxes. com*.

Example #2

My friend's mother was diagnosed with cancer and died within a few short months. As the end was nearing I started a Crowdfunding page for my friend (age 24) who was to become the sole guardian of her triplet siblings. Due to an amazing community effort, $36,000 was raised. All said it was a miracle...except when the 1099-K came in my name and I was told to claim the $36,000 as income. I cannot do this!

I did not get one cent of this money and my student loans are income based, so if the family even (very kindly) paid the taxes on the money, my *student loan payments would increase by $500 a month, something I just can't afford.*[45]

- Is there a problem?
- What do you see as a problem?
- How do you resolve the 1099-K issue?
- Is this income to the recipient? (What is the definition of a gift?)
- Is there a gift tax issue in this story?
- Is the recipient a 501(c)(3) organization?

Example #3:

I ran a successful crowdfunding campaign last year for a medical need (service animal) for my disabled daughter. It wouldn't be covered by insurance. It's a long process and we've paid a portion to the certified training company already. How do I need to file this for tax purposes?

I'm certain I need to file it as income, but with it being for a medical need is there any way to deduct the amount we've already paid?[46]

- How would you characterize the receipts: taxable? Gift? Why?
- If the taxpayer receives a 1099-K how should you report it?
- What about an excess of receipts over expenses? (medical care for his daughter, purchase and training of the service dog?)
- If the father received the funds and gives to his daughter, is there a gift tax issue?

Example #4

A client of mine recently became an amputee. A friend of his set up a Crowdfunding account to raise funds for the prosthetics and related medical costs. The friend had the funds, upward of $17,000, put into his own personal checking account instead of an account in my client's name. Well, the friend had back tax issues and the IRS levied the entire account. Gone. The obvious question is about recourse to see if the funds can be returned. My client contacted Crowdfunding to see if there was anything they *could do. Maybe with proof of recipient it could be overturned.*[47]

Example #5

On one crowdfunding site, two daughters raised more than $32,000 to pay for their mother's funeral costs after she died of spinal and brain cancer with a campaign titled "Goodbye Beautiful Mummy."[48]

- What tax issues do you see here?
- Are the donors' contributions tax deductible? What if they had a receipt?

Example #6

The "Rick and Kelly Schwab Memorial Fund" recently raised more than $23,000 on a crowdfunding to pay for the funerals of a couple killed on their motorcycle by an alleged drunk driver on July 4, leaving a 14 year-old son behind.[49]

- What tax issues do you see here?
- Are the donors' contributions tax deductible? What if they had a receipt?

- Are the extra contributions taxable to the 14 year-old son?
- What if the contributions were $230,000? While that change any answers?

Example #7:

"Two years after surviving a terrible car crash and battling cancer, Casey Charf never imagined she'd be fighting a new battle with the IRS. Paramedics flew Casey to the hospital after the crash near 276th and Bennington Road. During tests and scans to check for accident injuries, doctors discovered tumors hidden throughout Casey's body. She had no idea she had cancer. Hundreds of people in the Omaha metro area attended fundraisers for the Charf family to help with travel and medical expenses. Her sister also set up a crowdfunding account online, and more than a thousand people around the world donated to the Charfs, raising nearly $50,000. In the last two years, Casey has traveled to Maryland and Louisiana for treatment, and received chemotherapy and radiation here in Omaha as well. So far, efforts to find 'Casey's Cure'

have shown little progress; the cancer is still there. The IRS recently notified the Charfs that what they'd collected through crowdfunding should've been claimed as income. Of the nearly $50,000 the government wants $15,457 in back taxes, and another $3,676 in penalties and interest. In total, the letter indicates the Charfs owe the IRS $19,133 by April 29.)[50]

- What tax issues do you see here?
- What probably triggered the IRS to go after the taxes on this crowdfunding event?

(The IRS maintains the GoFundMe monies were taxable income. She is appealing the IRS position and it is the opinion of many tax professionals that Casey has a strong case. This may be the test case that is needed to determine the status of these "gifts." At a minimum, resolution of this case should help clarify the issue in these situations. Stay tuned.)[51]

Example #8

Memories Pizza owners Crystal O'Connor and her father, Kevin O'Connor were the subjects of a nationwide controversy after they told a local news station they were happy to serve gay people at their pizza shop, but if asked, they could not cater a same-sex wedding, because of their religious beliefs. That interview came during the national debate over Indiana's discriminatory anti-gay Religious Freedom Restoration Act. The backlash was swift, leading anti-gay conservatives directed by Rush Limbaugh to donate cash to support their religious beliefs, and to "ram it down" the throats of the LGBT community, as the boisterous right wing talk radio pundit demanded.[52] A third party opened a crowdfunding platform.[53] After four days, $842,387 was raised before the fundraiser mysteriously closed, no reason given.

Now, the O'Connors are speaking out again. They say they're ready to re-open for business after being "afraid" to open their door in light of the harassment they received. And they've decided what they're going to do with the proceeds of the fundraising campaign, which should, after fees, net them over three-quarters of a million dollars. The Daily Mail reports the O'Connors "are set to share their new fortune with disabled children, a women's help group, fire fighters, police trusts, Christian churches and Washington State florist Barronelle Stutzman, 70, who was fined after declaring she would not serve a gay wedding."[54]

- What tax issues do you see here?
- How should the funds be categorized? Taxable? Non-taxable? Why?
- The article states that the beneficiaries intend to "share their new fortune" with various groups and with an individual? What will be the nature of these shared amounts? What if the groups are not 501(c)(3) organizations?
- If a third party (creator) set up the account what would the tax consequences to the third party be for giving the collected funds to the recipients?
- If over $800,000 was collected why did the article talk about only three-quarters of a million dollars?

- What do you think was the original intent of the crowdfunding campaign?

Again, visit *www.crowdfundingtaxes.com* for discussion of these and other scenarios.

CROWD*FRAUD*ING

The problem with a concept like crowdfunding is that is potentially ripe for fraud because it depends upon trust. In the past a network of family and friends could vouch for a person's credibility before contributing. Today the creator is only as reliable as their promises. Unfortunately in this day and age, promises don't always deliver. Consider the following example.

The Federal Trade Commission recently settled a case against a project creator who scammed contributors out of more than $122,000. The creator, using a business name, was going to produce a board game designed by two prominent board-game artists. Over a period of 15 months, the creator provided periodic "updates." Then he announced he had cancelled the project. Although the creator had promised to refund contributions, he neither refunded the money nor provided any promised rewards. He had spent the money on rent, moving to another state, unrelated personal expenses and personal equipment and licenses for a different project.[55]

One of the "benefits" of using a crowdfunding platform may be providing press releases. But what list are they using? Is it a personalized list you provide or will it be the same list of 1,000s used over and over again? Consider the abilities of Facebook or Twitter? The original intent of these social media is about engaging and interacting with people. Do your own experiment. Do a Google search for "buy Twitter followers" or "buy Facebook likes." You can get 18,000 Twitter "followers" for $15 and 10,000 FB likes for just a little more. It looks great if you are trying to sell services but does nothing for reaching an audience for real crowdfunding promotion. [56]

While none of us believe we will be conned or that we can figure out the con, it really doesn't work that way. Maria Konnikova wrote a very interesting article, "Born to be Conned" where she gave example after example of trusting people who were conned.

One was a poor college student who arrived in New York City and upon seeing a man performing his version of the three-card monte quickly lost the only money she had brought, $40. She was frugal and intelligent (a student in sociology who would soon go on to get her Ph.D. and become a news editor at Scientific American. [57] Other examples are shared.

A physicist, who in 2011, fell for a sweetheart swindle on a dating website. Following what he thought was correspondence with a model, flew to South American for an in-person rendezvous, but ended up jailed for smuggling cocaine.

Maria writes that we become blind to inconsistencies that seem glaring in retrospect, well-told tales make red flags disappear. Faced with incongruous evidence, we dismiss the evidence rather than the story. Or perhaps, you don't dismiss it. You don't even see it. [58]

This article can be used as an aid or guide to help crowdfunding enthusiasts, especially those who could become donors or investors in a new, exciting crowdfunding offer.

AVOIDING
CROWDFUNDING SCAMS

Salvador Briggman wrote an article, "6 Ways to Avoid Crowdfunding Scams." Here are the "ways" and a brief explanation. The full article can be read online.[59]

1. **Google the project and the creator.**
   This is the *simplest* way that you can prevent being sucked into a scam.
   Before backing a project or paying a marketing company, look up what others have said about them on the web.

2. **Pinpoint unrealistic promises.**
   Unrealistic promises are usually an indication of one of two things:
   The creator hasn't correctly identified the costs of fulfilling their rewards or is overstating the value of the product.

The promise *is* too good to be true and the project is preying on your imagination or the hopes of what it could do or be.

3. **Verify need-based campaigns.**

   Need-based campaigns are typically on GoFundMe. The creator might be asking for help with medical bills, unexpected costs, or a horrible accident.

   It's disgusting, but some people do take advantage of the emotions around these types of events to scam donors.

   Unless it's one of your close friends, before donating money to a stranger's cause-related campaign, do your best to verify that the event *actually happened* and that all of the funds will go to the actual cause.

4. **Look into other backers.**

   Sometimes, a campaign will pay for backers or supporters to create the illusion that their project is trusted by others and that their product or cause is popular.

   These gigs are offered on Fiverr and other sites.

Before backing a project, do a quick google search of any images that the creator has uploaded to see if there are corresponding images on Alibaba or other sites.

5. **If the product is questionable, you can also always rely on the power of crowdsourcing and post it on the Kickstarter subreddit to see if anyone else recognizes it elsewhere on the web.**

6. **Report it.**

   Finally, if you think you've found a scam, report it! Here are a few places where you can do so:

   - Your state's Attorney General,[60]
   - the Federal Trade Commission-Complaint Assistant,[61] and
   - KickScammed.[62]

To help you learn more about the possibilities and probabilities of being scammed (or your clients being scammed), an interesting article about "7 Scam-tastic Crowdfunding Campaigns" should be a "must-read" on your list of continuing education. Among the crowdfunding list is the Kobe Red Beef Jerky. The story is about a creator who spins a story of beef jerky made from 100% Japanese Beer-fed Kobe Cows. The scam was quite well set up. Falsified comments were posted on the funding page stating how they enjoyed the jerky at their uncle's farm, another stated how they got a sample from a local event.[63] Another was an appeal by a supposed mother to send her daughter to a STEM (science, technology, engineering and mathematics) Camp. It did raise over $24,000.[64]

We have reviewed the history of the concept of crowdfunding. We have looked at the creative formation of how crowdfunding works. We have examined several crowdfunding stories to determine how these projects could be taxed. We have looked at the fraud side of crowdfunding. Now let's turn to the success side of crowdfunding – how it is supposed to work.

Sous-vide (French for "under vacuum") is a method of cooking in which food is sealed in airtight plastic bags then placed in a water bath or in a temperature-controlled steam environment for longer than normal cooking times (usually 1 to 6 hours, up to 48 or more in some select cases) at an accurately maintained temperature. It was commercially available for many years; however a team of people wanted to bring the methodology to the home kitchen affordably. The story of their success can be found in this story "Nomiku: bring sous vide into your kitchen" from June 18, 2012 to the present. [65] Their goal was to crowdfund $200,000 by offering an ascending ladder of rewards. Their goal was reached by July 18, 2012 successfully raising $586,061 with 1,880 backers. Their product is now available on Amazon, as is a competitor product, the Anova Precision Cooker. It raised $1,811,321 of their $100,000 goal in 42 days during June of 2014.

Another interesting story has to do with the development of a travel bag. It was described as a new backpack-meets-duffle-meets-carry on — a flashy 20-feature product. It launched July 19, 2016, with a goal of $20,000 but had raised $1.73 million with 9,067 backers by September 2, 2016. By the time the offering was closed it had raised $9.19 million. [66]

For those of you who, in moments of deep thought or contemplation repeatedly click a writing pen, here's a new idea for you. It's a widget…for fidget! They are about the size of a large die, and they come equipped with a bunch of fidgeting-friendly mechanisms on each side. There's stuff you can click, press, slide, roll, and spin. [67] Starting a crowdfunding project in August 2016 with a goal of $15,000, and using rewards for pledges, by mid-October 2016 they had received $5,770,657, with shipping to begin in December 2016. [68]

There have been unbelievable amounts of money raised by crowdfunding. A quick review of five outsized final results were featured in a story, "5 Kickstarter Projects Slammed with Success."[69]

Early in 2012 a slew of crowd-funded projects received money that was an order of magnitude more than request turning dreams into nightmares. Here is a summary of five of these crowdfunded projects.

Project	Funding Goal	Amount Received	Complications
Reprint 5,000 hardcover books of a web-comic about role-playing	$57,750	$1,254,120	The 110,000-book order exceeded the printer's capacity
Handmade screen prints	$3,000	$32,000	Hard to fulfill orders for 950 prints plus 660 hand-screened T-shirt bonus gifts
Inexpensive 3-D printing kits	$25,000	$839,827	IRS smacked creator with $330,000 bill
Offering smart watches that paired with iOS and Android phones	$100,000	$10,226,845	Wanted to make 1,000 watches, but had orders for 85,000
To produce a small run of sturdy, minimalist steel pens	$25,000	$281,989	Planned for 50, got orders for about 6,000 – received a cease-and-desist letter from alleged copyright holder and original manufacturer was incapable of meeting product specs

We have not covered all of the details regarding the topic of crowdfunding. We have left out a section regarding equity crowdfunding. This would be a process under which a private company could go "public" using the crowdfunding platform. Investopedia briefly describes the current process as follows:

"Going public refers to a private company's initial public offering (IPO), thus becoming a publicly traded and owned entity. Businesses usually go public to raise capital in hopes of expanding; venture capitalists may use IPOs as an exit strategy - that is, a way of getting out of their investment in a company.

The IPO process begins with contacting an investment bank and making certain decisions, such as the number and price of the shares that will be issued. Investment banks take on the task of underwriting, or becoming owners of the shares and assuming legal responsibility for them. The goal of the underwriter is to sell the shares to the public for more than what was paid to the original owners of the company. Deals between investment banks and issuing companies can be valued at hundreds of millions of dollars, some even hitting $1 billion.

Going public does have positive and negative effects, which companies must consider. Here are a few of them:

- *Advantages* - Strengthens capital base, makes acquisitions easier, diversifies ownership, and increases prestige.
- *Disadvantages* - Puts pressure on short-term growth, increases costs, imposes more restrictions on management and on trading, forces disclosure to the public, and makes former business owners lose control of decision making.

For some entrepreneurs, taking a company public is the ultimate dream and mark of success (usually because there is a large payout). However, before an IPO can even be discussed, a company must meet requirements laid out by the underwriters. Here are some characteristics that may qualify a company for an IPO:

- High growth prospects
- Innovative product or service
- Competitive in industry
- Able to meet financial audit requirements

Some underwriters require revenues of approximately $10-$20 million per year with profits around $1 million! Not only have that, but management teams should show future growth rates of about 25% per year in a five- to seven-year span. While there are exceptions to the requirements, there is no doubt over how much hard work entrepreneurs must put in before they collect the big rewards of an IPO."[70]

As you can see, for a small business this process is prohibitively expensive. It is similar to the process of going through an angel or venture capital or a commercial bank. Recognizing this Congress began in 2011 crafting legislation intended to encourage funding of United States small businesses by easing various securities regulations. It passed with bipartisan support, and was signed into law by President Barack

Obama on April 5, 2012. The Jumpstart Our Business Startup Act of 2012 or "The JOBS Act" is also sometimes used informally to refer to just Titles II and III of the legislation which are the two most important pieces to much of the equity crowdfunding and startup community. Title II went into effect on September 23, 2013. On October 30, 2015, the SEC adopted final rules allowing Title III equity crowdfunding. The final rules and forms went into effect on May 16, 2016. [71]

Just the summary of the JOBS Act is over seven pages long. Perhaps it is the topic for another booklet on another day.

Hopefully this material will bring the reader up to a common level of knowledge of the "pros and cons" of crowdfunding and the many, many income tax challenges this subject brings to the tax table.

For further insights and information, including links to all sources referenced herein, visit the Crowdfunding and Taxes companion website at *www.crowdfundingtaxes.com*

ENDNOTES

1   Armstrong, Casey. "What Is Crowdfunding? - Daily Crowdsource." *Daily Crowdsource*. Web. 16 Jan. 2016. <http://dailycrowdsource.com/ training/crowdfunding/what-is-crowdfunding>.

2   "The History of Crowdfunding." *The History of Crowdfunding*. Startups.co. Web. 16 Jan. 2016. <https://www.fundable.com/crowdfunding101/ history-of-crowdfunding>.

3   Neiss, S., Best, J. W., & Cassady-Dorion, Z. (n.d.). Crowdsourcing versus Crowdfunding: What Is the Difference ... Retrieved October 20, 2016, from http://www.dummies.com/ personal-finance/investing/crowdfund-in-vesting/crowdsourcing-versus-crowdfund-ing-what-is-the-difference/

4   Kazmark, Justin. "Kickstarter Before Kickstarter." *Kickstarter*. Kickstarter Blog, 18 July 2013. Web. 16 Jan. 2016. <https://www.kickstarter. com/blog/kickstarter-before-kickstarter>.

5   Ibid.

6   ibid.

7   Ibid.

8   Freedman, David M, and Matthew R Nutting.
        "A Brief History of Crowdfunding: Including
        Rewards, Donation, Debt, and Equity Plat-
        forms in the USA." *History-of-Crowdfunding.
        pdf.* Financial Poise, 5 Nov. 2015. Web. 16 Jan.
        2016. <http://www.freedman-chicago.com/
        ec4i/History-of-Crowdfunding.pdf>.

9   Avampato, Christa. "Angel, VC, Crowd-
        funding, or Bootstrap?" *Triple Pundit People
        Planet Profit*, Triple Pundit, 17 Sept. 2015,
        http://www.triplepundit.com/2012/09/an-
        gel-vc-crowdfunding-bootstrap-funding-mod-
        el/.

10   Armstrong, Casey. "What Is Crowdfunding? -
        Daily Crowdsource." *Daily Crowdsource.* Web.
        16 Jan. 2016. <http://dailycrowdsource.com/
        training/crowdfunding/what-is-crowdfunding>.

11   Adams, Susan. "Ten of the Best Businesses
        to Come Out Of Shark Tank." *Forbes*, Forbes
        Magazine, 18 May 2016, http://www.forbes.
        com/sites/susanadams/2016/03/18/ten-of-the-

best-businesses-to-come-out-of-shark-tank/
print/.

12   "Choose Your Funding Type: Can I Keep
My Money?" *Indiegogo Help Center*, https://
support.indiegogo.com/hc/en-us/arti-
cles/205138007-choose-your-funding-type-
can-i-keep-my-money-.

13   Hurst, Samantha. "Researchers Study Indiegogo's Flexible or Fixed Crowdfunding
- Crowdfund Insider." *Crowdfund Insider ICal*,
24 June 2014, https://www.crowdfundinsider.
com/2014/06/42609-researchers-study-indi-
egogos-flexible-or-fixed-crowdfunding/.

14   Briggman, Salvador. "What Are the Pros and
Cons of Crowdfunding?" *Crowdfunding Success
Tips What Are the Pros and Cons of Crowdfunding Comments*, Crowd Crux, http://www.
crowdcrux.com/pros-and-cons-of-crowdfund-
ing/. Blog

15   Knipp, Kirsten. "Benefits and Drawbacks of
Crowdfunding - The BigCommerce Blog." *The
BigCommerce Blog*, https://www.bigcommerce.
com/blog/benefits-and-drawbacks-of-crowd-
funding/. Blog

16 "The Pros and Cons of Crowdfunding Your New Business." *Learn Finance Online*, http://www.globalfinanceschool.com/blog-post/pros-and-cons-crowdfunding-your-new-business.

17 ibid.

18 ibid.

19 "Royalty Crowdfunding Definition." *EquityNet*, https://www.equitynet.com/crowdfunding-terminology/royalty-crowdfunding.

20 Salman, SH. "The Global Crowdfunding Industry Raised $34.4 Billion In 2015, And Could Surpass VC In 2016 - Dazeinfo." *Dazeinfo*, 12 Jan. 2016, http://dazeinfo.com/2016/01/12/crowdfunding-industry-34-4-billion-surpass-vc-2016/.

21 "Crowd Funding Presents a New Area of Tax Planning Expertise." *Crowd Funding Presents a New Area of Tax Planning Expertise.* InvestmentNews, 30 Jan. 2013. Web. 16 Jan. 2016. <http://www.investmentnews.com/article/20130130/FREE/130139993/crowd-funding-presents-a-new-area-of-tax-planning-expertise>.

22 Long, Thomas M. "Federal Tax Issues Associ-

ated with 'Crowdfunding'." *AccountingWEB*, 16 Dec. 2015, http://www.accountingweb.com/tax/individuals/federal-tax-issues-associated-with-crowdfunding.

23   Salman. <u>supra</u>.

24   Mercado, Darla. "Crowd Funding Presents a New Area of Tax Planning Expertise." *Crowd Funding Presents a New Area of Tax Planning Expertise*. InvestmentNews, 30 Jan. 2013. Web. 16 Jan. 2016. <http://www.investmentnews.com/article/20130130/FREE/130139993/crowd-funding-presents-a-new-area-of-tax-planning-expertise>.

25   Duchman, Zalmi. "The On-Demand Economy Is Here To Stay, And Now Is The Time To Put It To Use For Your Business." *Forbes*, Forbes Magazine, 14 July 2015, http://www.forbes.com/sites/zalmiduchman/2015/07/14/the-on-demand-economy-is-here-to-stay-and-now-is-the-time-to-put-it-to-use-for-your-business/#1a5a305443f8.

26   "Small Business/Self-Employed Topics." *Sharing Economy Tax Center*, US Government Publishing, 19 Sept. 2016, https://www.irs.gov/

businesses/small-businesses-self-employed/sharing-economy-tax-center.

27 www.sharedeconomycpa.com

28 "Crowdfunding." *The TaxBook WebLibrary*, The TaxBook, http://thetaxbook.net/occupations-lifestyles-2015/page-13-1. Subscription Required

29 "Top 10 Crowdfunding Sites." *By Traffic Rank*. GoFundMe. Web. 16 Jan. 2016. <http://www.crowdfunding.com/>.

30 Recomendes, Joe. "How Much Does It Cost to Run a Crowdfunding Campaign?" *Command Partners*, http://commandpartners.com/blog/how-much-does-it-cost-to-run-a-crowdfunding-campaign. Blog

31 "Form 1099-MISC, Miscellaneous Income." *Form 1099-MISC, Miscellaneous Income*, US Government Publishing, https://www.irs.gov/uac/about-form-1099misc.

32 Erb, Kelly Phillips. "Credit Cards, The IRS, Form 1099-K And The $19,399 Reporting Hole." *Forbes*, Forbes Magazine, 8 Aug. 2014, http://www.forbes.com/sites/kellyphillipserb/2014/08/29/credit-cards-the-

irs-form-1099-k-and-the-19399-reporting-hole/#6e3c0ec96c37.

33   Form 1099-MISC, supra.

34   Dunn, Jennifer. "Tax Form 1099-K: The Lowdown for Amazon FBA Sellers." *TaxJar Sales Tax Blog*, TaxJar, 27 Jan. 2016, http://blog.taxjar.com/1099-k-amazon-fba/. Blog

35   Erb, "Credit Cards", supra.

36   Ibid.

37   "Crowdfunding." *The TaxBook WebLibrary,* supra

38   Ibid.

39   Ibid.

40   ibid

41   ibid.

42   Zollars, Ed. "Tax Aspects of Crowdfunding Discussed in IRS Information Letter." *Current Federal Tax Developments*, Nichols Patrick CPE, Incorporated, 30 June 2016, http://www.currentfederaltaxdevelopments.com/blog/2016/6/30/tax-aspects-of-crowdfunding-discussed-in-irs-information-letter.

43   Fitzpatrick, JD, Diana. "50-State Guide to Internet Sales Tax Laws | Nolo.com." Nolo.com.

Nolo.com. Web. 16 Jan. 2016. <http://www. nolo.com/legal-encyclopedia/50-state-guide-in- ternet-sales-tax-laws.html>.

44   Herigstad, Sally. "5 Things to Know About Crowdfunding and Taxes - TaxAct Blog." *TaxAct Blog*, TaxAct, http://blog.taxact.com/5- things-know-crowdfunding-taxes/. Blog

45   Rhode, Steve. "My Crowdfunding Donations to Help a Sick Friend Are 1099-K Taxable In- come?" *Get Out of Debt Guy*. Myvesta Founda- tion, 4 Feb. 2015. Web. 16 Jan. 2016.

46   "How to Claim Crowdfunding Campaigns on Tax Return." *TaxAct Blog*, http://blog.taxact. com/crowdfunding/.

47   Reams, II, Lee. "How an IRS Bank Levy Turned a Go Fund Me Campaign Into a Night- mare." *How an IRS Bank Levy Turned a Go Fund Me Campaign Into a Nightmare*. TaxBuzz, 18 Aug. 2015. Web. 16 Jan. 2016. <http:// www.taxbuzz.com/blog/how-an-irs-bank-levy- turn-a-go-fund-me-campaign-into-a-night- mare>.

48   Kulp, Kayleigh. "Crowdfunding Funerals: What You Need To Know." *Fox Business*, 8

Aug. 2014, http://www.foxbusiness.com/
features/2014/08/08/crowdfunding-funerals-
what-need-to-know.html.

49 ibid.

50 Peterson, Brandi. "IRS: Cancer Survivor Owes
$19,000 in Taxes from Donations." KETV,
KETV7ABC, 27 Apr. 2015, http://www.ketv.
com/news/irs-cancer-survivor-owes-19000-in-
taxes-from-donations/32584500.

51 Stancil. Supra,

52 Erb, Kelly Phillips. "Crowdfunding Raises
$800,000 For Memories Pizza Parlor: What
It Means For Donors &Amp; Future Campaigns." *Forbes*, Forbes Magazine, 7 Apr.
2015, http://www.forbes.com/sites/kellyph-
illipserb/2015/04/07/crowdfunding-raises-
800000-for-memories-pizza-parlor-what-it-
means-for-donors-future-campaigns/.

53 Moyer, Justin Wm. "Conservative Commen-
tator Lawrence B. Jones behind Crowdfunding
for Ind. Pizza Shop That Won't Cater Gay
Wedding." *Washington Post*, The Washington
Post, 6 Apr. 2015, https://www.washington-
post.com/news/morning-mix/wp/2015/04/06/

indiana-pizza-shop-gofundme-page-set-up-by-glenn-beck-news-site/.

54   Bhatia, Shekhar. "EXCLUSIVE: 'If a Child of Mine Was Gay I Would Love Them, but I Still Wouldn't Go to the Wedding.' Defiant Indiana Pizza Parlor Owners Who Won't Cater for Gay Receptions REOPEN Store Tomorrow, Buoyed by Donations of $842,000." *Mail Online*, Associated Newspapers, 7 Apr. 2015, http://www.dailymail.co.uk/news/article-3028925/if-child-gay-love-wouldn-t-wedding-defiant-indiana-pizza-parlor-owners-won-t-cater-gay-reception-reopen-store-today-buoyed-donations-842-000.html.

55   Fredman, Catherine. "Fund Me or Fraud Me? Crowdfunding Scams Are on the Rise." *Consumer Reports*. Consumer Reports, 5 Oct. 2015. Web. 16 Jan. 2016. <http://www.consumerreports.org/cro/money/crowdfunding-scam>.

56   Hogue, Joseph. "Are Crowdfunding Promotion Services a Scam? [And What to Do]." *Crowd 101*, Crowd101.Com, 5 Oct. 2016, http://www.crowd101.com/crowdfunding-promotion-scam/.

57 Konnikova, Maria. "Born to Be Conned." *The New York Times*, The New York Times, 5 Dec. 2015, http://www.nytimes.com/2015/12/06/opinion/sunday/born-to-be-conned.html.

58 Ibid.

59 Briggman, Salvador. "6 Ways to Avoid Crowdfunding Scams." *Crowdfunding Success Tips 6 Ways to Avoid Crowdfunding Scams Comments*. Salvador Briggman, LLC, 31 Aug. 2015. Web. 16 Jan. 2016. <http://www.crowdcrux.com/ways-to-avoid-crowdfunding-scams/>.

60 "National Association of Attorneys General." NAAG, NAAG, http://www.naag.org/naag/attorneys-general/whos-my-ag/virginia/mark-herring.php.

61 "FTC Complaint Assistant." *FTC Complaint Assistant*, Federal Trade Commission, https://www.ftccomplaintassistant.gov/#crnt.

62 "Report Crowdfunding Scams." *Kickscammed*, KickStarter, Inc., http://kickscammed.com/.

63 "7 Scam-tastic Crowdfunding Campaigns." *Best Gadgets*. Gadget Review, 7 Jan. 2014. Web. 16 Jan. 2016. <http://www.gadgetreview.com/7-scamtastic-crowdfunding-campaigns>.

64 ibid.

65 Fetterman, Lisa Q. "Nomiku: Bring Sous Vide into Your Kitchen." Kickstarter, *KickStarter*, Inc., 17 Mar. 2015, https://www.kickstarter.com/projects/nomiku/nomiku-bring-sous-vide-into-your-kitchen.

66 Kussin, Zachary. "This Bag Will Change the Way You Travel." *New York Post*, 20 July 2016, http://nypost.com/2016/07/20/this-bag-will-change-the-way-you-travel/.

67 Flynn, Conner. "Fidget Cube Is Heaven for Fidgeters." *Technabob*, The Awesomer, 6 Sept. 2016, http://technabob.com/blog/2016/09/06/fidget-cube-toy-for-fidgeting/.

68 McLachlan, Matthew, and Mark McLachlan. "Fidget Cube: A Vinyl Desk Toy." *Kickstarter*, KickStarter, Inc., https://www.kickstarter.com/projects/antsylabs/fidget-cube-a-vinyl-desk-toy. Blog

69 "5 Kickstarter Projects Slammed With Success." *Wired.com*. Conde Nast Digital, 26 June 2012. Web. 16 Jan.2016. <http://www.wired.com/2012/07/st_kickstarter/?viewall=true>.

70 Staff, Investopedia. "What Does 'Going

Public' Mean?" *Investopedia*, http://www.
investopedia.com/ask/answers/04/061704.asp.
Investopedia Encyclopedia

71 "Jumpstart Our Business Startups Act." *Wikipedia*, Wikimedia Foundation, 5 Oct. 2016,
https://en.wikipedia.org/wiki/jumpstart_our_
business_startups_act.

Morgan James Speakers Group

We connect Morgan James published
authors with live and online events
and audiences who will benefit
from their expertise.

Morgan James makes all of our titles available through the Library for All Charity Organization.

www.LibraryForAll.org

Printed in the USA
CPSIA information can be obtained
at www.ICGtesting.com
JSHW080004150824
68134JS00021B/2270